Susan B. Anthony

A Photo-Illustrated Biography
by Lucile Davis

Content Consultant:
Andrea Libresco
Department of Curriculum and Teaching
Hofstra University

Bridgestone Books
an imprint of Capstone Press

Facts about Susan B. Anthony

- Susan B. Anthony was a leader in the fight for women's rights.
- Elizabeth Cady Stanton was another women's rights leader. Susan met Elizabeth in 1851. They worked together for 51 years.
- In 1872, police arrested Susan for trying to vote. At the time, women were not allowed to vote.

Bridgestone Books are published by Capstone Press
818 North Willow Street, Mankato, Minnesota 56001 • http://www.capstone-press.com
Copyright ©1998 by Capstone Press. All rights reserved. No part of this book may be reproduced in any form without written permission from the publisher. The publisher takes no responsibility for the use of any of the materials or methods described in this book, nor for the products thereof.
Printed in the United States of America.

Library of Congress Cataloging-in-Publication Data
Davis, Lucile.
  Susan B. Anthony: a photo-illustrated biography/by Lucile Davis.
    p. cm.--(Read and discover photo-illustrated biographies)
  Includes bibliographical references (p. 24).
Summary: An introductory biography of the early women's rights activist who fought for women's right to vote.
  ISBN 1-56065-750-2
  1. Anthony, Susan B. (Susan Brownell), 1820-1906--Juvenile literature. 2. Feminists
--United States--Biography--Juvenile literature. 3. Suffragists--United States--Biography--Juvenile literature.
4. Women--Suffrage--United States--History--Juvenile literature. [1. Anthony, Susan B. (Susan Brownell),
1820-1906. 2. Feminists. 3. Women--Biography.] I. Title. II. Series.
HQ1413.A55D38 1998
305.42'092--dc21
[B]   97-41651
                                                         CIP
                                                          AC

Editorial Credits
Editor, Greg Linder; cover design, Timothy Halldin; photo research, Michelle L. Norstad

Photo Credits
Archive Photos, cover, 4, 10; Corbis-Bettmann, 8, 12, 16, 20; Department of Rare Books and Special Collections, University of Rochester Library, 6; Schlesinger Library, Radcliffe College, 14, 18

Table of Contents

Leader and Guide 5

Early Years 7

School Teacher 9

Susan Meets Elizabeth 11

A Petition for Rights 13

Slavery and Equal Rights 15

The Revolution 17

Woman Suffrage 19

The 19th Amendment 21

Words from Susan B. Anthony 22

Important Dates in Susan B. Anthony's Life 23

Words to Know 23

Read More 24

Useful Addresses and Internet Sites 24

Index 24

Leader and Guide

Susan Brownell Anthony was an American women's rights leader. She guided the struggle for women's rights in the 1800s. She believed women should have the same rights as men.

Susan was a Quaker. Quakers are members of a Christian group founded in 1650. Christians are people who follow the teachings of Jesus Christ. Quakers oppose all war. They believe that men and women should be treated equally.

Both men and women spoke at Quaker meetings in the 1800s. Only men could speak at most churches.

At that time, women could not vote. They could not hold government offices. Married women could not own property or sue people in court. Most colleges would not accept women as students.

Susan knew this was not fair. She met other women who felt the same way. She spent most of her life working for women's rights.

Susan B. Anthony spent her life working for women's rights.

Early Years

Susan B. Anthony was born February 15, 1820, in Adams, Massachusetts. Her father Daniel ran a cotton mill. Her mother Lucy raised eight children. Susan's father was a Quaker. Her mother was not. Susan became a Quaker at age 13.

Susan learned to read and write by the age of five. She wanted to learn math. The school master would not teach math to girls. So Susan taught herself.

Susan's father hired young women to work in his mill. Many of the women stayed at the Anthony home. They worked 12 hours a day. Susan's mother worked even longer. She cooked and cleaned for the family during the day. At night, she cooked for the women who worked at the mill.

Susan helped her mother. She could cook an entire dinner by the age of ten. She understood that running a household was hard work.

Susan became a Quaker like her father Daniel.

School Teacher

Susan's father believed education was important. Daniel taught classes for the mill workers at night. He sent Susan to an advanced school for girls. She was 17. But Daniel's business failed a year later.

Susan became a teacher to help support her family. She taught at a school in New York.

In 1846, Susan became the head teacher for girls. The head teacher for boys at the school was a man. He earned more money than Susan because he was a man. She knew this was not fair. But she did not know what to do about it.

Susan's parents attended a women's rights meeting in 1850. They told Susan about laws that were unfair to women. A year later, Susan decided to quit teaching. Instead, she would work to change unfair laws. She started working for women's rights.

Susan quit teaching in 1851. She started working to change laws that were unfair to women.

Susan Meets Elizabeth

Susan met Elizabeth Cady Stanton in 1851. Elizabeth had planned the first women's rights convention in 1848. A convention is a meeting of people with the same interests. The women's rights convention took place in Seneca Falls, New York.

Susan and Elizabeth became friends for life. They made a good team. Susan was a good speaker and a good planner. Elizabeth was a powerful speaker and writer. They started working to win equal rights for women.

Elizabeth made speeches and wrote articles. Her words helped people understand the need for women's rights. Susan set up meetings. Her plans guided people in their work.

Elizabeth was married. She was also busy raising seven children. She could not be away from home very often. Susan never married. She could travel freely and speak about women's rights.

Susan and Elizabeth Cady Stanton became friends for life.

A Petition for Rights

Susan and Elizabeth created a petition in 1854. A petition is a letter signed by many people. Petitions often ask for changes in the law. Ten thousand people signed Susan and Elizabeth's petition.

Susan and Elizabeth presented their petition to the New York legislature. A legislature is a group of people that makes laws. The petition asked legislators to give women equal rights.

Elizabeth gave a powerful speech. Most legislators respected what she had to say. But they did not do what the women asked. Susan told the legislators she would be back.

Susan returned to the legislature with more petitions. In 1860, legislators finally passed a new law. It gave married women in New York the right to own property. Single women already had that right. Women still did not have the same rights as men. But the new law was a beginning.

This cartoon shows Elizabeth speaking to the New York legislature. She asked legislators to give women equal rights.

Slavery and Equal Rights

Susan and Elizabeth also fought against slavery. They believed that no one should own another person. They started a women's group to help end slavery.

Susan created another petition. About 400,000 people signed this petition. Susan presented it to the United States Congress in 1864. Congress makes laws for the entire country.

Congress passed the 13th Amendment to the U.S. Constitution in 1865. An amendment is a change made to a law. The 13th Amendment ended slavery in the United States. Susan's petition helped Congress decide to pass the amendment.

Congress passed the 14th Amendment in 1868. It granted rights to men who were once slaves. But these men could not vote. Women did not have the right to vote either. Susan and Elizabeth began working to win equal rights for all people.

Susan's petition helped Congress decide to end slavery.

The Revolution

In 1868, Susan and Elizabeth started a newspaper. It was called *The Revolution.*

Articles in the newspaper explained the need for equal rights. Susan and Elizabeth also printed articles about other subjects. They printed articles about education, business, marriage, and women's history.

Susan raised money to print the newspaper. Elizabeth wrote many articles. As many as 3,000 readers paid to receive the newspaper.

Congress passed the 15th Amendment to the U.S. Constitution in 1870. It gave African-American men the right to vote. The amendment did not give women this right. Many women were disappointed.

Susan and Elizabeth stopped printing *The Revolution* in 1870. The newspaper owed $10,000 to printers and other people. Susan promised to pay the $10,000 with her own money. She finished paying six years later.

Susan and Elizabeth started a newspaper called *The Revolution.*

Woman Suffrage

Susan traveled across the United States. She gave speeches about the need for woman suffrage. Suffrage is the right to vote.

Susan decided to break the law by voting in 1872. A police officer arrested her. In court, a judge fined her $100. Susan refused to pay the fine. Instead, she gave a speech about woman suffrage.

Susan and Elizabeth wrote three books about woman suffrage. The first book was published in 1881. It was called *A History of Woman Suffrage.*

In 1888, Susan planned a meeting for women from many nations. Women came to the United States from Europe and Asia. The meeting helped bring worldwide attention to women's rights.

Susan and Elizabeth became leaders of a woman suffrage group. Elizabeth was president. Susan guided the work of the group. Susan continued leading the group after Elizabeth died in 1902.

Susan planned a meeting for women from many nations in 1888.

The 19th Amendment

In 1906, Susan spoke at a national woman suffrage meeting. She asked women to keep working for the right to vote. Susan died one month later.

Susan had prepared other women to work for women's rights. They took up the fight. In 1920, Congress passed the 19th Amendment. Many people called it the Susan B. Anthony Amendment. It gave women the right to vote.

An artist named Adelaide Johnson created a statue. The statue shows Elizabeth, Susan, and Lucretia Mott. Lucretia was another women's rights leader. The artist gave the statue to the United States in 1921. It now stands in the Capitol building in Washington, D.C. The statue honors the women who worked for equal rights.

The U. S. government honored Susan many years later. The government put her picture on a coin. The Susan B. Anthony dollar first appeared in 1979.

Artist Adelaide Johnson created this statue of Elizabeth, Susan, and Lucretia Mott.

Words from Susan B. Anthony

"Still another form of slavery remains to be disposed of; the old idea yet prevails that woman is owned and possessed by man."

From a speech by Susan B. Anthony. She spoke in Kansas at the close of the Civil War.

"The most ignorant and degraded man who walks to the polls feels himself superior to the most intelligent woman."

From a speech, 1894

"Failure is impossible."

A statement Susan made at her 86th birthday party. She believed women could not fail if they kept working for women's rights.

"Men, their rights and nothing more.
Women, their rights and nothing less."

Motto of *The Revolution,* the newspaper started by Susan and Elizabeth Cady Stanton.

Important Dates in Susan B. Anthony's Life

1820—Born February 15 in Adams, Massachusetts
1838—Becomes a school teacher to help support her family
1851—Meets Elizabeth Cady Stanton
1854—Presents a petition for women's rights to the New York state legislature
1864—Presents a petition opposing slavery to the U.S. Congress
1868—Starts a newspaper called *The Revolution*
1872—Is arrested after voting
1902—Susan's friend Elizabeth Cady Stanton dies
1906—Susan dies in Rochester, New York

Words to Know

amendment (uh-MEND-muhnt)—a change made to a law
Christian (KRISS-chun)—a follower of the teachings of Jesus Christ
Congress (KONG-griss)—the part of the U.S. government that makes laws for the whole country
convention (kuhn-VEN-shun)—a meeting of people with the same interests
legislature (LEJ-iss-lay-chur)—a group of people that makes laws
petition (puh-TISH-uhn)—a letter signed by many people
Quaker (KWAY-kur)—a member of a Christian group founded in 1650
suffrage (SUF-ruhj)—the right to vote

Read More

Cooper, Ilene. *Susan B. Anthony*. New York: Franklin Watts, 1984.

Fritz, Jean. *You Want Women to Vote, Lizzie Stanton?* New York: G.P. Putnam's Sons, 1995.

Harvey, Miles. *Women's Voting Rights*. Cornerstones of Freedom. Danbury, Conn.: Children's Press, 1996.`

Levin, Pamela. *Susan B. Anthony*. Junior World Biographies. Broomall, Penn.: Chelsea House Publishers, 1993.

Useful Addresses and Internet Sites

Susan B. Anthony Home
17 Madison Street
Rochester, NY 14608

Women's Rights National Historical Park
136 Fall Street
Seneca Falls, NY 13148

Encyclopedia of Women's History
http://www.teleport.com/~megaines/women.html
Welcome to the Susan B. Anthony House!
http://www.frontiernet.net/~lhurst/sbahouse/sbahome.htm

Index

amendment, 15, 17, 21
Congress, 15, 17, 21
convention, 11
legislature, 13
Mott, Lucretia, 21
petition, 13, 15
Quaker, 5, 7
Revolution, The, 17

Seneca Falls, 11
slavery, 15
Stanton, Elizabeth Cady, 11, 13, 15, 17, 19, 21
statue, 21
suffrage, 19, 21
teacher, 9
women's rights, 5, 9, 11, 19, 21